Kakuro
for Kids

Ninja Edition

Alastair Chisholm

Walker & Company

NEW YORK

First published in the United States of America in 2006 by
Walker Publishing Company, Inc.
Distributed to the trade by Holtzbrinck Publishers

For information about permission to reproduce selections from
this book, write to Permissions, Walker & Company,
104 Fifth Avenue, New York, New York 10011

ISBN-10: 0-8027-9606-0
ISBN-13: 978-0-8027-9606-6

Book design by Esy Casey

Visit Walker & Company's Web site at www.walkeryoungreaders.com

Printed in the United States of America

2 4 6 8 10 9 7 5 3 1

All papers used by Walker & Company are natural, recyclable products
made from wood grown in well-managed forests. The manufacturing processes
conform to the environmental regulations of the country of origin.

Welcome to Kakuro for Kids!

In this book are some of the most interesting and diabolical puzzles around, puzzles so hard they'll make your brain bulge. They're fiendish and terrifying, but don't worry; with enough clues, practice and patience, you too can be a Kakuro Master! Are you ready to be a Black Belt in Kakuro?

What is Kakuro?

Kakuro is a logic puzzle from Japan. It's based on an empty grid with some helpful clues. The aim is to use the clues to fill the grid with all the missing numbers. Kakuro puzzles come in all shapes and sizes.

Here's an example:

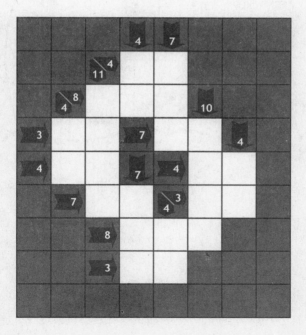

It looks a bit like a crossword puzzle, doesn't it?
Here it is again:

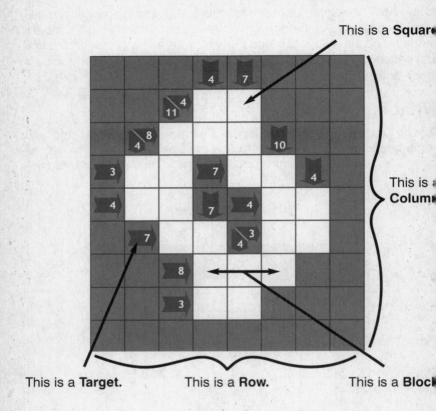

This is a **Square**

This is a **Column**

This is a **Target.**   This is a **Row.**   This is a **Block**

A Kakuro puzzle is made up of Blocks of white Squares.

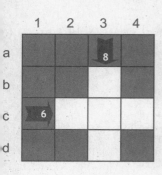

There are two Blocks here, one going Across and the other going Down.

Look at the arrows at the top and the left of the Blocks. The arrows tell you the Target for each Block. To solve the puzzle, the numbers in the Block have to add up to the Target.

So, the Down Block has a Target of **8**, and three Squares.

That's Rule #1 of Kakuro:

Rule #1: The numbers in each Block add up to the Block's Target.

There's only one other rule in Kakuro, which is this:

Rule #2: You can't use a number twice in the same Block.

We'll come back to Rule #2 later. In the meantime, here are the same Blocks, with some of the answers filled in.

What number do you think should go into Square **c3** (Row **c**, Column **3**)?

If you add up the numbers we've found so far in the Across Block **(1 + 3)**, it comes to **4**. The **Target** for the Across Block is **6**—so the missing number must be a **2**, like this:

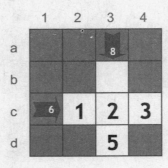

Let's try that again. There's only one empty Square left in the Down Block. The numbers we've found in the Down Block **(2 + 5)** come to **7**, and the Target is **8**, so the last Square must be a **1**.

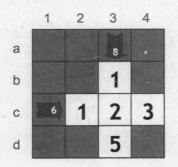

Believe it or not, you've just solved your first Kakuro puzzle!

When there are Blocks with only one Square to be solved, we call it the **Last Man Left**. Looking for the Last Man Left Squares is one trick to help you crack the grid. There are some other tricks for solving Kakuro puzzles, and we'll explain them later on.

Kakuro puzzles can be real brain stretchers, but don't worry; you'll get the hang of them pretty quickly. Before you know it, you'll be adding up Rows and Columns without a moment's thought. To help you along, we've arranged this book into **five levels**:

THE 5 KAKURO BELT LEVELS

White Belt: Some fun and easy, cozy puzzles to warm up your brain.

Yellow Belt: A little harder, but full of tips and tricks to help you along.

Green Belt: A real workout—you'll have to be at your best with these opponents!

Brown Belt: Silent and deadly!

Black Belt: H I I I - Y A !
The ultimate challenge, for true Kakuro masters only—you have been warned!

To start things off, here are a few White Belt puzzles. We've added some clues, so all you need to do for now is remember Rule #1—

Rule #1: The numbers in each Block add up to the Block's Target.

(You don't need to worry about Rule #2 for these White Belt puzzles—but you will later!)

Good luck, and we'll meet again if you make it past White Belt!

Alastair

White Belt

Ninja Notes

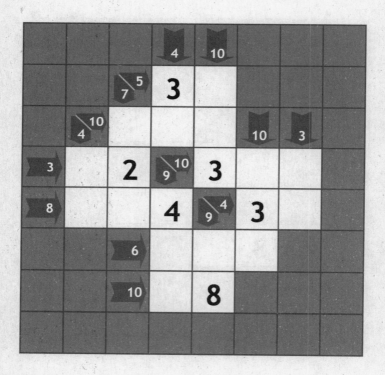

Target	Number of Squares	Combination
3	2	1, 2
4	2	1, 3
6	3	1, 2, 3
7	3	1, 2, 4
10	4	1, 2, 3, 4

Ninja Notes

Target	Number of Squares	Combination
3	2	1, 2
4	2	1, 3
6	3	1, 2, 3
7	3	1, 2, 4
10	4	1, 2, 3, 4

Ninja Notes

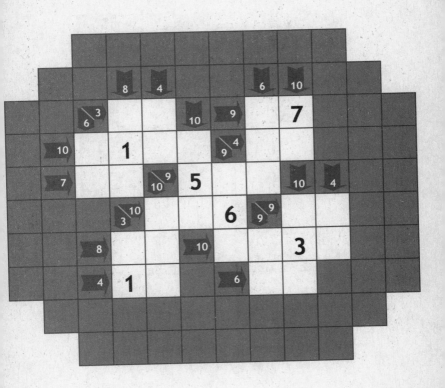

Target	Number of Squares	Combination
3	2	1, 2
4	2	1, 3
6	3	1, 2, 3
7	3	1, 2, 4
10	4	1, 2, 3, 4

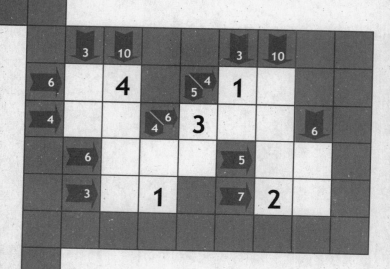

Target	Number of Squares	Combination
3	2	1, 2
4	2	1, 3
6	3	1, 2, 3
7	3	1, 2, 4
10	4	1, 2, 3, 4

Ninja Notes

Kakuro for Kids

PART TWO: Enter if You Dare!

Back so soon, eh? You must be ready to try something a bit harder!

In the warm-up White Belt puzzles, you had lots of clues to help you out. But a real Kakuro board doesn't have *any* clues. How on earth would you know how to start?

The trick is to think about Rule #2. Remember it? Here it is again:

Rule #2: You can't use a number twice in the same Block.

Believe it or not, with just this second rule and a few handy tricks, you can solve every puzzle in the rest of this book. Here's how it works. Look at the board, below:

The Block going Down from **g5** has a Target of **4** and two Squares to work with. In Kakuro, the trick is to think about all the ways we could add up the Target **4**. Here's the whole list:

$$1 + 3 = 4$$
$$2 + 2 = 4$$
$$3 + 1 = 4$$

But wait—**Rule #2** says we can't use the same number twice. We can't have **2 + 2**, because that would use 2 twice. So actually, our list is:

$$1 + 3 = 4$$
$$3 + 1 = 4$$

(By the way, when our Block has a Target of **4**, and two Squares, we call it a **4-in-2**.)

We've narrowed things down quite a bit. We know for a *fact* that Square g5 must be either a **1** or a **3**. Which one is it? Read on . . .

Kakuro Blocks

4-in-2 is actually a very useful Block; it's what we call a **Kakuro Block**. Kakuro Blocks have only one possible set of numbers. For example, for **4-in-2** we've seen that the values are 1 and 3—nothing else fits. Here are the most basic Kakuro Blocks:

To reach 3 with two Squares	(**3-in-2**)	use 1 and 2
To reach 4 with two Squares	(**4-in-2**)	use 1 and 3
To reach 6 with three Squares	(**6-in-3**)	use 1, 2 and 3
To reach 7 with three Squares	(**7-in-3**)	use 1, 2 and 4
To reach 10 with four Squares	(**10-in-4**)	use 1, 2, 3 and 4

There are more, but you don't need to worry about them just yet. Of course, we don't know the order the numbers go in yet—we don't know if our **4-in-2** is 1 + 3 or 3 + 1. This is where the really clever Kakuro stuff comes in, and here's the first step—Hot Spots.

Hot Spots

A Hot Spot is the Square where two Blocks cross, and have only one possible value in common. Look at the board again:

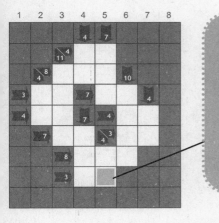

The **4-in-2** crosses another Kakuro Block, a **3-in-2**. We know that **4-in-2** must be made up of 1 and 3. And from our list, we know that **3-in-2** must be made up of 1 and 2. And that means they have only one number in common—1—so 1 must be in the Square where they cross!

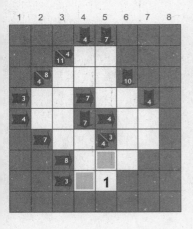

Starting from nothing, we've found one of the numbers already. And we can fill in some more now as well. You should be able to work out what the values are in Squares **g5** and **h4**, too. Can you?

This board has more Hot Spots—see how far you can solve it. When you've reached as far as you can, read on!

Locked Values

By looking for Hot Spots, and by using the Last Man Left trick to fill in Squares, you can get this far:

That's pretty good! But what can we do now?

The answer is **Locking**. This is where you look for Blocks that are partly solved, and try to work out where the remaining numbers must go. It helps if you know what the numbers are! Luckily, we can use Kakuro Blocks to help us out. Look at the board again:

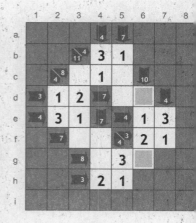

d6 is a **10-in-4** (remember, that means it has a Target of 10 and four Squares).

That's great news, because **10-in-4** happens to be a Kakuro Block! (Have a look back at the list on the previous page to check.) That means there's only one set of numbers that fits:

$1 + 2 + 3 + 4 = 10$.

We've already found 1 and 2. Let's look at 3. Could it be in **d6**? Well . . . yes, as far as we know.

Could it be in **g6**?
In fact, the 3 can't be in **g6**, because there's already a 3 in that Row. Remember **Rule #2**—

Rule #2: You can't use a number twice in the same Block.

So we know now that the 3 has to go into Square **d6** instead. And that means that **g6** has to be the 4.

Let's try that again with another example:

> **f4** is a **7-in-3**, which is another Kakuro Block. The only numbers that work are 1 + 2 + 4 = 7. We've found 2, so we have 1 and 4 left. Let's see where 4 could be.
>
> Could it be in **f4**? Sure, as far as we know. What about **g4**?
>
> **g4** is in the same Block as the 4 we just found in the last example. You can't have a number twice in the same Block, so . . . the 4 *can't* go into **g4**. It must be back in **f4**. We've solved another Square!

So now you know about Last Man Left, Kakuro Blocks, Hot Spots and Locking, and you're ready to go. As a quick warm-up, why not finish off the puzzle above? If you get stuck, you can look at the solution for Puzzle 11.

For added fun, see if you can guess the shape each puzzle forms. Some of them are freestyle creations, but others form shapes and objects. Check your guesses in the Solutions section.

Don't Guess!

It's tempting, isn't it? When you're stuck, and it could be 3 or 4, yo
think, "Well, let's just try and see . . . " But don't do it! Before long you
lovely, clean puzzle will be a mass of scribbled ink and crossed ou
numbers. You'll have totally lost track of which numbers are right an
which ones were guesses; and your brain will feel like someone jus
reached into your head and squeezed really hard.

Trust me. Every puzzle in this book can be solved with logic—tha
means you can always work out the next step if you think long and har
enough. But once you start guessing, you're guaranteed to end u
confused. So don't guess!

Make Notes

By now you've probably figured out that Kakuro is all about *combinations*
If you had a Target of 8 and three Squares, what numbers would fit
How many different ways can you add up 12 from four Squares? You'
be amazed how quickly you get the hang of this once you start doin
a lot of puzzles. But sometimes you're bound to get stuck—I still do!

When I start to lose track of where I am, I just write down a few notes a
the side of the page. For example, suppose I am looking at a **12-in-4**
(Remember, that's when you have a Target of 12 and four Squares.
I might write this down:

12-in-4

Then I think of all the combinations I can make that would fit. If I make
a mistake, I just cross it out. Then when I look at the puzzle again,
don't have to remember everything. Give it a try!

1 + 2 + 3 + 6

1 + 3 + 4 + 5

~~1 + 4 + 5 + 6~~

More Complicated Blocks

In the examples for Locked Values, we were lucky enough to find Kakuro Blocks each time. That means we found blocks where we knew *what* the numbers were, even if we weren't sure *where* they went.

For many of the puzzles in this book, that will be enough, but sometimes it won't be so neat. What if there is more than one possible solution? What if it's an **8-in-3**, for example? Then the numbers could be 1 + 2 + 5 = 8, or 1 + 3 + 4 = 8—which one is right?

When this happens, don't panic! Keep looking. First, there may be a useful Kakuro Block you haven't found yet. Then, think about each combination in turn. Would it fit? Would it stop something else from fitting? You'll be surprised—almost all the time, there's only one combination that fits, even if the Block isn't a Kakuro Block.

Make notes to keep track of situations like this, and after a while you'll find you don't need to.

On Your Mark . . . Get Set . . .

The puzzles in the rest of the book are going to get tougher, but don't worry—we've put some clues in to help you along. With every level you reach, the puzzles will get harder, and once you've mastered the dreaded Black Belt level, you will truly be a Kakuro Master. Other kids will fear and respect you, doctors will be amazed at how large your brain has become, you will be able to move objects using only the power of your mind and soon you will RULE THE WORLD.*

Good luck!

Alastair

This may not actually happen. But it would be pretty cool, wouldn't it?

Kakuro Blocks—A Handy List

In the introduction, we showed you some of the most frequently used Kakuro Blocks—that is, Blocks with only one combination that fits. Here's a full list of all the Kakuro Blocks that could appear in this book. Don't worry if you have to keep referring back to it—pretty soon you'll find you'll have memorized the whole thing!

TARGET	NUMBER OF SQUARES	COMBINATION	CALLED
3	2	1, 2	(3-in-2)
4	2	1, 3	(4-in-2)
16	2	7, 9	(16-in-2)
17	2	8, 9	(17-in-2)
6	3	1, 2, 3	(6-in-3)
7	3	1, 2, 4	(7-in-3)
23	3	6, 8, 9	(23-in-3)
24	3	7, 8, 9	(24-in-3)
10	4	1, 2, 3, 4	(10-in-4)
11	4	1, 2, 3, 5	(11-in-4)
29	4	5, 7, 8, 9	(29-in-4)
30	4	6, 7, 8, 9	(30-in-4)
15	5	1, 2, 3, 4, 5	(15-in-5)
16	5	1, 2, 3, 4, 6	(16-in-5)
34	5	4, 6, 7, 8, 9	(34-in-5)
35	5	5, 6, 7, 8, 9	(35-in-5)

Yellow Belt

Yellow 11 Belt

Target	Number of Squares	Combination
3	2	1, 2
4	2	1, 3
6	3	1, 2, 3
7	3	1, 2, 4
10	4	1, 2, 3, 4
11	4	1, 2, 3, 5

Ninja Notes

Target	Number of Squares	Combination
3	2	1, 2
4	2	1, 3
6	3	1, 2, 3
7	3	1, 2, 4
10	4	1, 2, 3, 4
11	4	1, 2, 3, 5

Ninja Notes

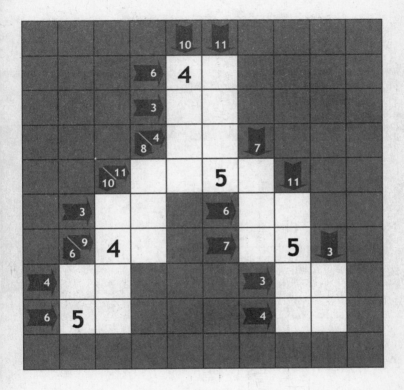

Yellow 16 Belt

Target	Number of Squares	Combination
3	2	1, 2
4	2	1, 3
6	3	1, 2, 3
7	3	1, 2, 4
10	4	1, 2, 3, 4
11	4	1, 2, 3, 5

Ninja Notes

Yellow · 17 · Belt

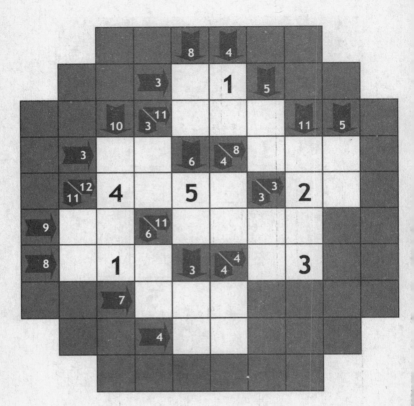

Target	Number of Squares	Combination
3	2	1, 2
4	2	1, 3
6	3	1, 2, 3
7	3	1, 2, 4
10	4	1, 2, 3, 4
11	4	1, 2, 3, 5

Target	Number of Squares	Combination
3	2	1, 2
4	2	1, 3
6	3	1, 2, 3
7	3	1, 2, 4
10	4	1, 2, 3, 4
11	4	1, 2, 3, 5

Target	Number of Squares	Combination
3	2	1, 2
4	2	1, 3
6	3	1, 2, 3
7	3	1, 2, 4
10	4	1, 2, 3, 4
11	4	1, 2, 3, 5

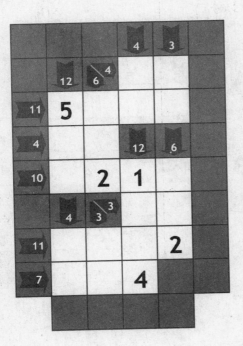

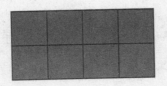

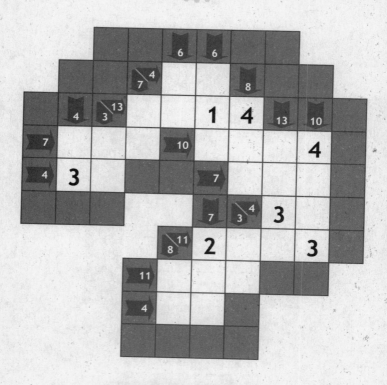

Target	Number of Squares	Combination
3	2	1, 2
4	2	1, 3
6	3	1, 2, 3
7	3	1, 2, 4
10	4	1, 2, 3, 4
11	4	1, 2, 3, 5

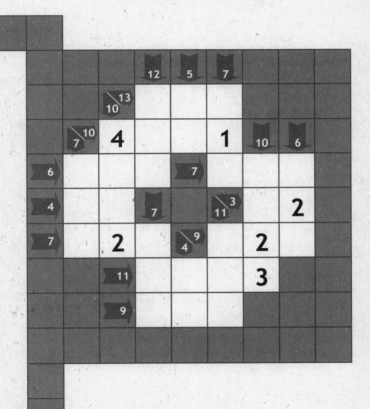

Green Belt

Green 26 Belt

Target	Number of Squares	Combination
3	2	1, 2
4	2	1, 3
6	3	1, 2, 3
7	3	1, 2, 4
10	4	1, 2, 3, 4
11	4	1, 2, 3, 5
15	5	1, 2, 3, 4, 5

Ninja Notes

Green 27 Belt

Green 28 Belt

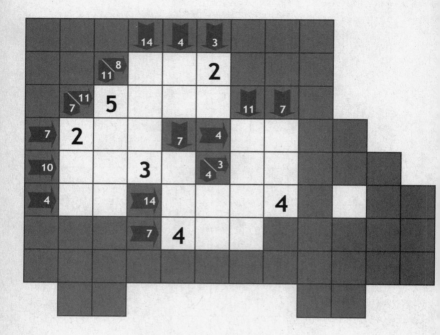

| | Number of | |
Target	Squares	Combination
3	2	1, 2
4	2	1, 3
6	3	1, 2, 3
7	3	1, 2, 4
10	4	1, 2, 3, 4
11	4	1, 2, 3, 5
15	5	1, 2, 3, 4, 5

Ninja Notes

Green 29 Belt

Green 30 Belt

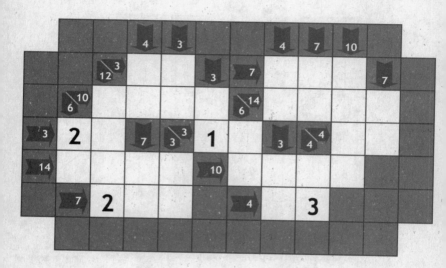

Ninja Notes

Green 32 Belt

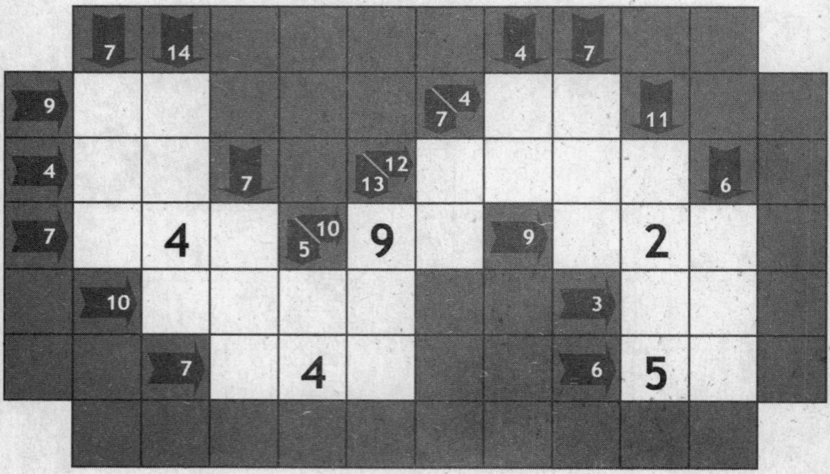

Target	Number of Squares	Combination
3	2	1, 2
4	2	1, 3
6	3	1, 2, 3
7	3	1, 2, 4
10	4	1, 2, 3, 4
11	4	1, 2, 3, 5
15	5	1, 2, 3, 4, 5

Ninja Notes

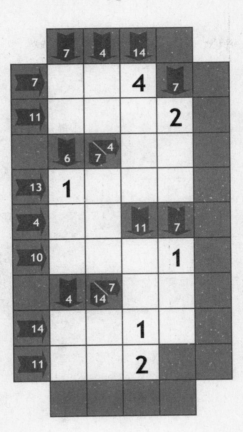

Green 34 Belt

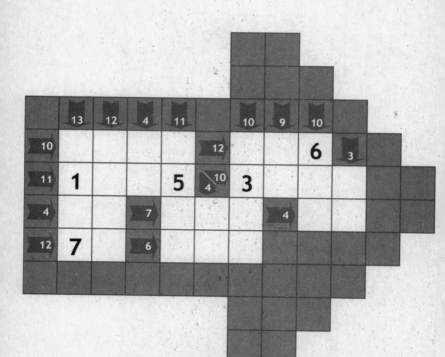

Ninja Notes

Green 35 Belt

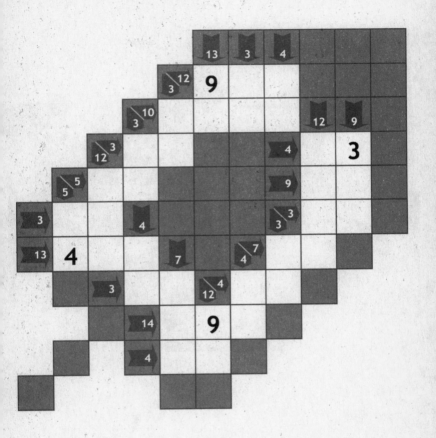

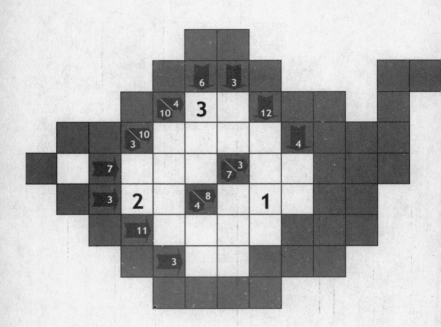

Ninja Notes

Target	Number of Squares	Combination
3	2	1, 2
4	2	1, 3
6	3	1, 2, 3
7	3	1, 2, 4
10	4	1, 2, 3, 4
11	4	1, 2, 3, 5
15	5	1, 2, 3, 4, 5

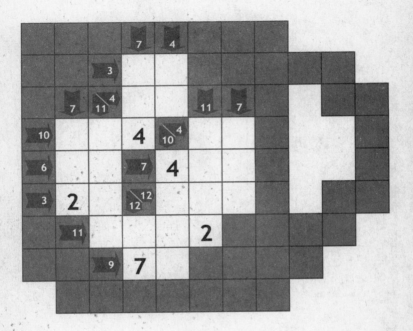

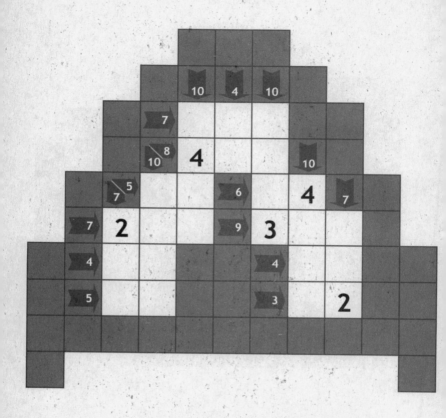

Target	Number of Squares	Combination
3	2	1, 2
4	2	1, 3
6	3	1, 2, 3
7	3	1, 2, 4
10	4	1, 2, 3, 4
11	4	1, 2, 3, 5
15	5	1, 2, 3, 4, 5

Ninja Notes

Green 40 Belt

Ninja Notes

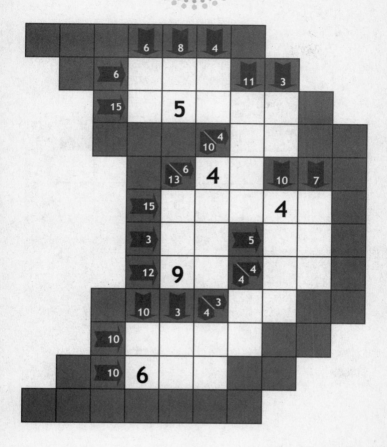

Ninja Notes

Target	Number of Squares	Combination
3	2	1, 2
4	2	1, 3
6	3	1, 2, 3
7	3	1, 2, 4
10	4	1, 2, 3, 4
11	4	1, 2, 3, 5
15	5	1, 2, 3, 4, 5

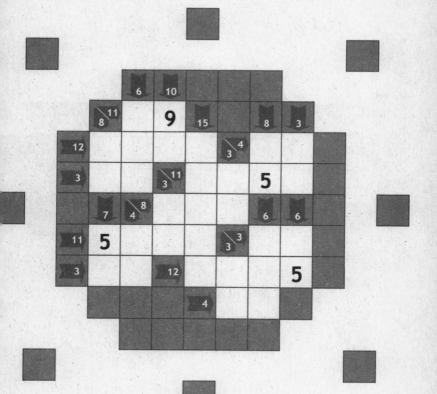

Green 44 Belt

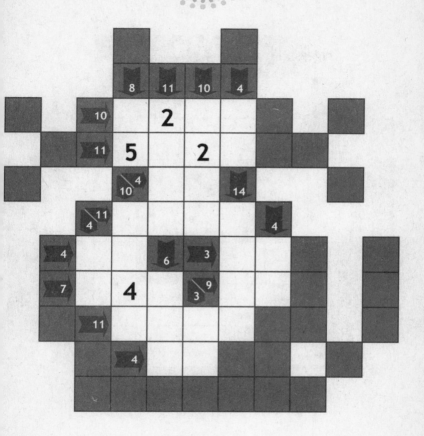

Target	Number of Squares	Combination
3	2	1, 2
4	2	1, 3
6	3	1, 2, 3
7	3	1, 2, 4
10	4	1, 2, 3, 4
11	4	1, 2, 3, 5
15	5	1, 2, 3, 4, 5

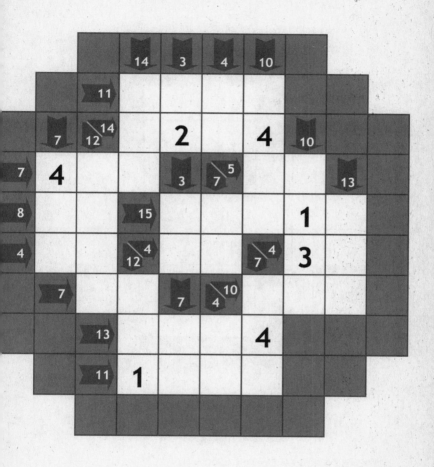

Green **48** Belt

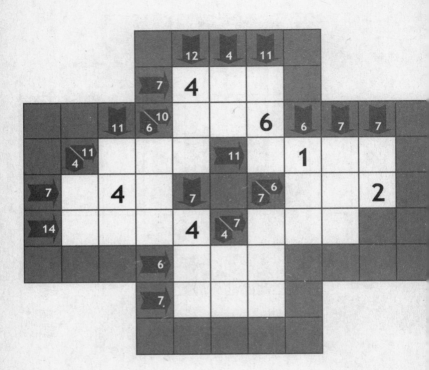

Target	Number of Squares	Combination
3	2	1, 2
4	2	1, 3
6	3	1, 2, 3
7	3	1, 2, 4
10	4	1, 2, 3, 4
11	4	1, 2, 3, 5
15	5	1, 2, 3, 4, 5

			6 ↓	8 ↓	3 ↓	7 ↓		
		10 →	**1**			**4**	10 ↓	
	12 ↓	10\15 →						
8 →					4 →			4 ↓
9 →	**7**		7 ↓			10\3 →		
	4 →			4 ↓	8\11 →	**7**		
	15 →							
		10 →		**1**				

Target	Number of Squares	Combination
3	2	1, 2
4	2	1, 3
6	3	1, 2, 3
7	3	1, 2, 4
10	4	1, 2, 3, 4
11	4	1, 2, 3, 5
15	5	1, 2, 3, 4, 5

Ninja Notes

Green 52 Belt

Target	Number of Squares	Combination
3	2	1, 2
4	2	1, 3
6	3	1, 2, 3
7	3	1, 2, 4
10	4	1, 2, 3, 4
11	4	1, 2, 3, 5
15	5	1, 2, 3, 4, 5

Green **53** Belt

Green 54 Belt

Ninja Notes

Target	Number of Squares	Combination
3	2	1, 2
4	2	1, 3
6	3	1, 2, 3
7	3	1, 2, 4
10	4	1, 2, 3, 4
11	4	1, 2, 3, 5
15	5	1, 2, 3, 4, 5

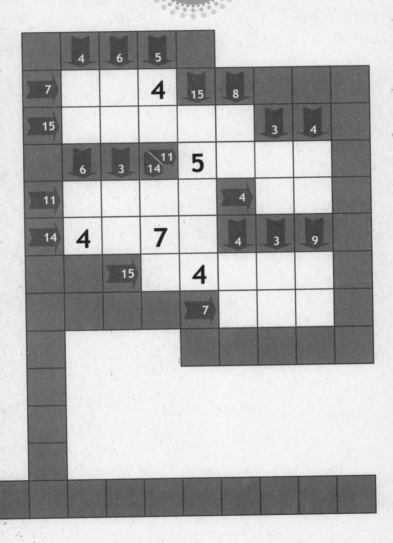

Brown Belt

Target	Number of Squares	Combination
3	2	1, 2
4	2	1, 3
16	2	7, 9
17	2	8, 9
6	3	1, 2, 3
7	3	1, 2, 4
10	4	1, 2, 3, 4
11	4	1, 2, 3, 5
15	5	1, 2, 3, 4, 5
16	5	1, 2, 3, 4, 6

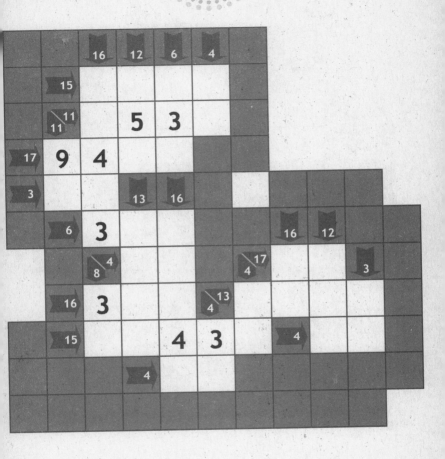

Brown 58 Belt

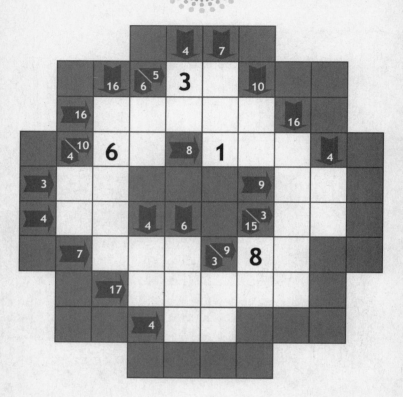

Target	Number of Squares	Combination
3	2	1, 2
4	2	1, 3
16	2	7, 9
17	2	8, 9
6	3	1, 2, 3
7	3	1, 2, 4
10	4	1, 2, 3, 4
11	4	1, 2, 3, 5
15	5	1, 2, 3, 4, 5
16	5	1, 2, 3, 4, 6

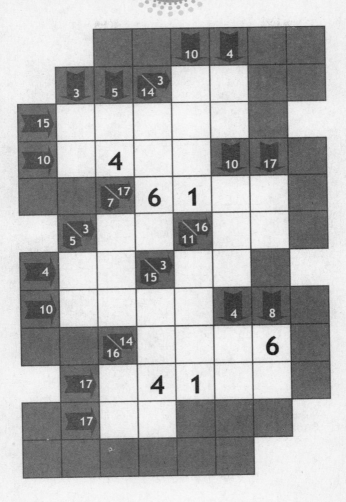

Brown 60 Belt

	Number of	
Target	Squares	Combination
3	2	1, 2
4	2	1, 3
16	2	7, 9
17	2	8, 9
6	3	1, 2, 3
7	3	1, 2, 4
10	4	1, 2, 3, 4
11	4	1, 2, 3, 5
15	5	1, 2, 3, 4, 5
16	5	1, 2, 3, 4, 6

Ninja Notes

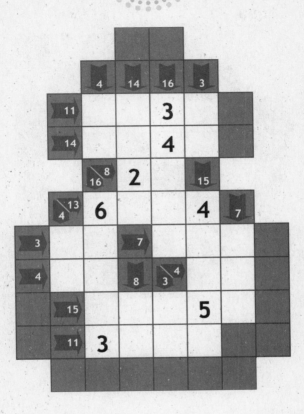

Brown 62 Belt

Target	Number of Squares	Combination
3	2	1, 2
4	2	1, 3
16	2	7, 9
17	2	8, 9
6	3	1, 2, 3
7	3	1, 2, 4
10	4	1, 2, 3, 4
11	4	1, 2, 3, 5
15	5	1, 2, 3, 4, 5
16	5	1, 2, 3, 4, 6

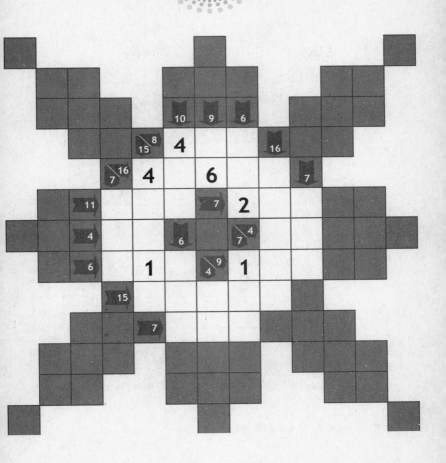

Brown 64 Belt

Ninja Notes

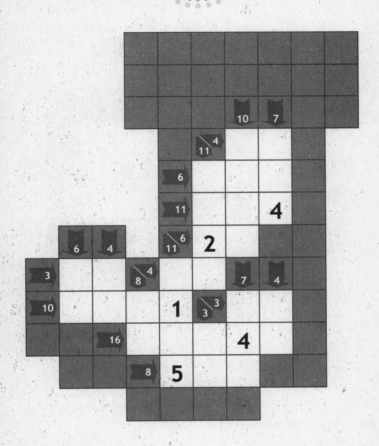

Brown 66 Belt

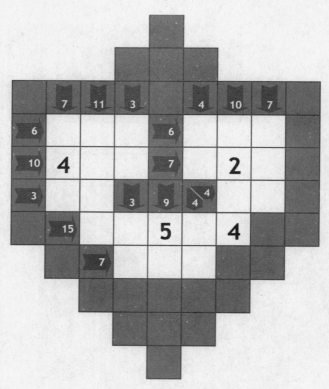

Target	Number of Squares	Combination
3	2	1, 2
4	2	1, 3
16	2	7, 9
17	2	8, 9
6	3	1, 2, 3
7	3	1, 2, 4
10	4	1, 2, 3, 4
11	4	1, 2, 3, 5
15	5	1, 2, 3, 4, 5
16	5	1, 2, 3, 4, 6

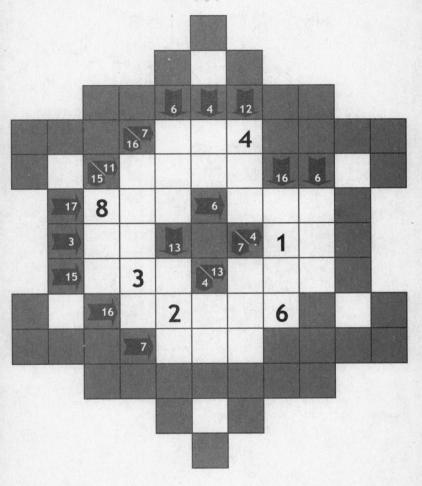

Target	Number of Squares	Combination
3	2	1, 2
4	2	1, 3
16	2	7, 9
17	2	8, 9
6	3	1, 2, 3
7	3	1, 2, 4
10	4	1, 2, 3, 4
11	4	1, 2, 3, 5
15	5	1, 2, 3, 4, 5
16	5	1, 2, 3, 4, 6

Ninja Notes

Target	Number of Squares	Combination
3	2	1, 2
4	2	1, 3
16	2	7, 9
17	2	8, 9
6	3	1, 2, 3
7	3	1, 2, 4
10	4	1, 2, 3, 4
11	4	1, 2, 3, 5
15	5	1, 2, 3, 4, 5
16	5	1, 2, 3, 4, 6

Ninja Notes

Brown 71 Belt

Brown 72 Belt

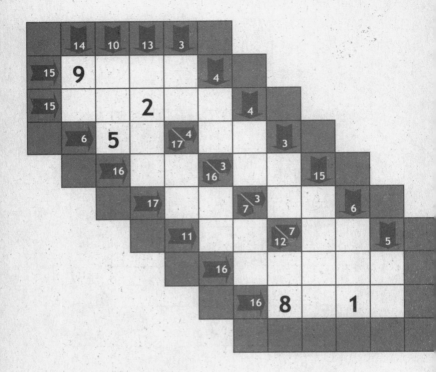

Target	Number of Squares	Combination
3	2	1, 2
4	2	1, 3
16	2	7, 9
17	2	8, 9
6	3	1, 2, 3
7	3	1, 2, 4
10	4	1, 2, 3, 4
11	4	1, 2, 3, 5
15	5	1, 2, 3, 4, 5
16	5	1, 2, 3, 4, 6

Ninja Notes

Brown 74 Belt

Target	Number of Squares	Combination
3	2	1, 2
4	2	1, 3
16	2	7, 9
17	2	8, 9
6	3	1, 2, 3
7	3	1, 2, 4
10	4	1, 2, 3, 4
11	4	1, 2, 3, 5
15	5	1, 2, 3, 4, 5
16	5	1, 2, 3, 4, 6

Brown 76 Belt

Target	Number of Squares	Combination
3	2	1, 2
4	2	1, 3
16	2	7, 9
17	2	8, 9
6	3	1, 2, 3
7	3	1, 2, 4
10	4	1, 2, 3, 4
11	4	1, 2, 3, 5
15	5	1, 2, 3, 4, 5
16	5	1, 2, 3, 4, 6

Ninja Notes

Brown 78 Belt

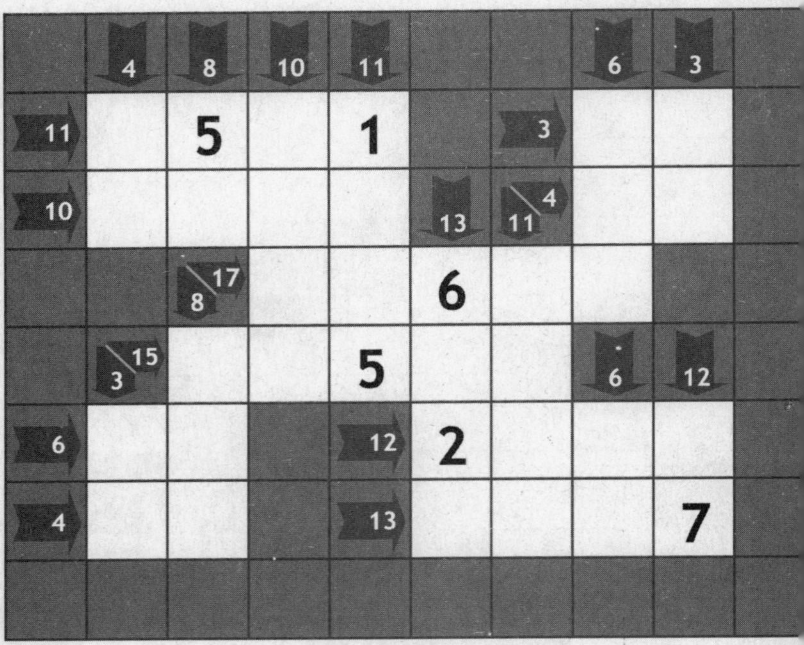

Target	Number of Squares	Combination
3	2	1, 2
4	2	1, 3
16	2	7, 9
17	2	8, 9
6	3	1, 2, 3
7	3	1, 2, 4
10	4	1, 2, 3, 4
11	4	1, 2, 3, 5
15	5	1, 2, 3, 4, 5
16	5	1, 2, 3, 4, 6

Ninja Notes

Brown 80 Belt

Ninja Notes

Brown 81 Belt

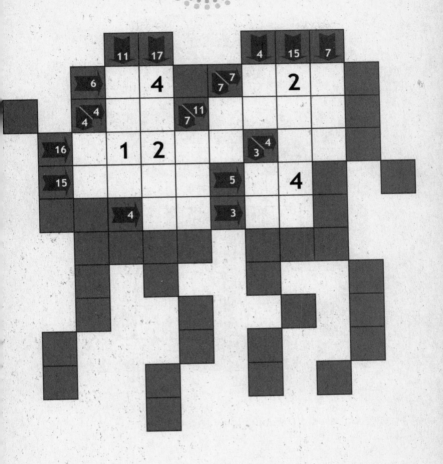

Target	Number of Squares	Combination
3	2	1, 2
4	2	1, 3
16	2	7, 9
17	2	8, 9
6	3	1, 2, 3
7	3	1, 2, 4
10	4	1, 2, 3, 4
11	4	1, 2, 3, 5
15	5	1, 2, 3, 4, 5
16	5	1, 2, 3, 4, 6

Ninja Notes

Target	Number of Squares	Combination
3	2	1, 2
4	2	1, 3
16	2	7, 9
17	2	8, 9
6	3	1, 2, 3
7	3	1, 2, 4
10	4	1, 2, 3, 4
11	4	1, 2, 3, 5
15	5	1, 2, 3, 4, 5
16	5	1, 2, 3, 4, 6

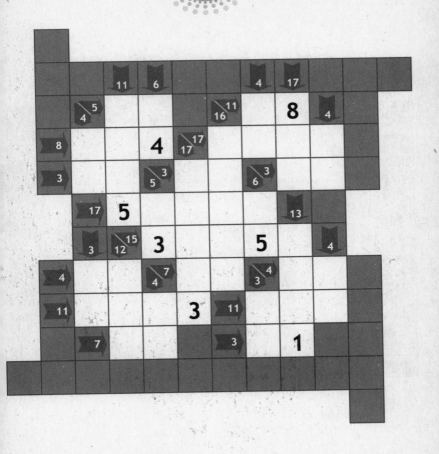

Brown 86 Belt

Target	Number of Squares	Combination
3	2	1, 2
4	2	1, 3
16	2	7, 9
17	2	8, 9
6	3	1, 2, 3
7	3	1, 2, 4
10	4	1, 2, 3, 4
11	4	1, 2, 3, 5
15	5	1, 2, 3, 4, 5
16	5	1, 2, 3, 4, 6

Ninja Notes

Brown 88 Belt

Target	Number of Squares	Combination
3	2	1, 2
4	2	1, 3
16	2	7, 9
17	2	8, 9
6	3	1, 2, 3
7	3	1, 2, 4
10	4	1, 2, 3, 4
11	4	1, 2, 3, 5
15	5	1, 2, 3, 4, 5
16	5	1, 2, 3, 4, 6

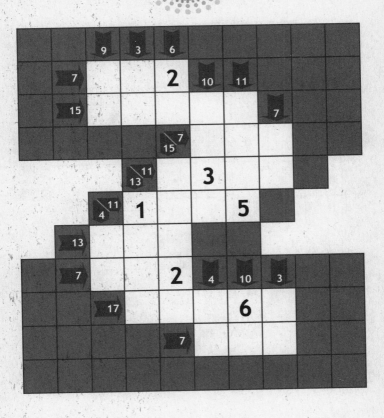

Brown 90 Belt

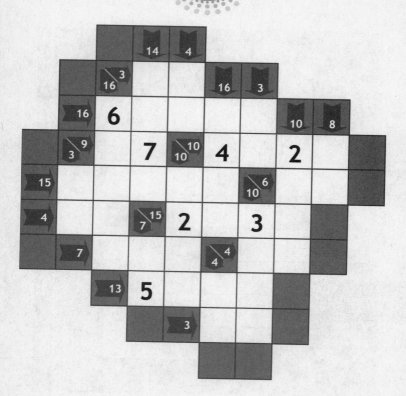

Target	Number of Squares	Combination
3	2	1, 2
4	2	1, 3
16	2	7, 9
17	2	8, 9
6	3	1, 2, 3
7	3	1, 2, 4
10	4	1, 2, 3, 4
11	4	1, 2, 3, 5
15	5	1, 2, 3, 4, 5
16	5	1, 2, 3, 4, 6

Black Belt

Target	Number of Squares	Combination
3	2	1, 2
4	2	1, 3
16	2	7, 9
17	2	8, 9
6	3	1, 2, 3
7	3	1, 2, 4
23	3	6, 8, 9
24	3	7, 8, 9
10	4	1, 2, 3, 4
11	4	1, 2, 3, 5
29	4	5, 7, 8, 9
30	4	6, 7, 8, 9
15	5	1, 2, 3, 4, 5
16	5	1, 2, 3, 4, 6
34	5	4, 6, 7, 8, 9
35	5	5, 6, 7, 8, 9

Ninja Notes

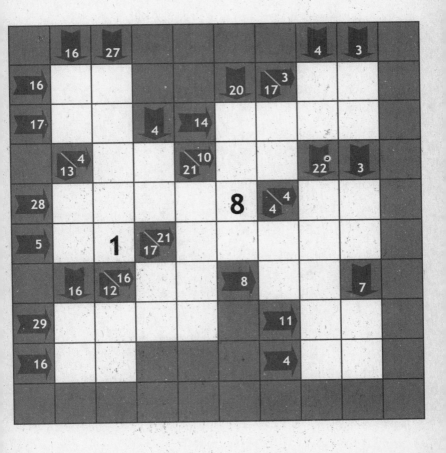

Target	Number of Squares	Combination
3	2	1, 2
4	2	1, 3
16	2	7, 9
17	2	8, 9
6	3	1, 2, 3
7	3	1, 2, 4
23	3	6, 8, 9
24	3	7, 8, 9
10	4	1, 2, 3, 4
11	4	1, 2, 3, 5
29	4	5, 7, 8, 9
30	4	6, 7, 8, 9
15	5	1, 2, 3, 4, 5
16	5	1, 2, 3, 4, 6
34	5	4, 6, 7, 8, 9
35	5	5, 6, 7, 8, 9

Ninja Notes

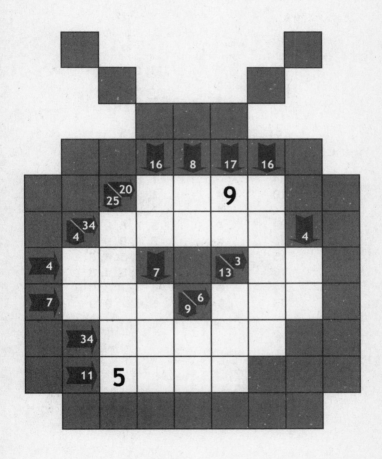

Target	Number of Squares	Combination
3	2	1, 2
4	2	1, 3
16	2	7, 9
17	2	8, 9
6	3	1, 2, 3
7	3	1, 2, 4
23	3	6, 8, 9
24	3	7, 8, 9
10	4	1, 2, 3, 4
11	4	1, 2, 3, 5
29	4	5, 7, 8, 9
30	4	6, 7, 8, 9
15	5	1, 2, 3, 4, 5
16	5	1, 2, 3, 4, 6
34	5	4, 6, 7, 8, 9
35	5	5, 6, 7, 8, 9

Ninja Notes

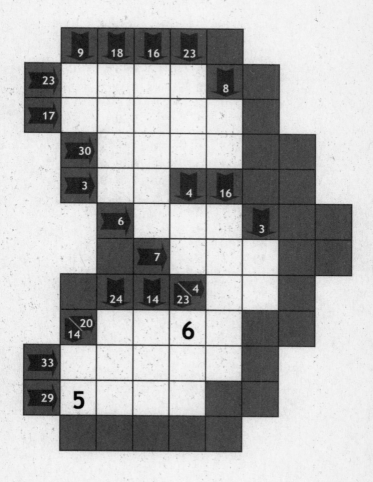

Target	Number of Squares	Combination
3	2	1, 2
4	2	1, 3
16	2	7, 9
17	2	8, 9
6	3	1, 2, 3
7	3	1, 2, 4
23	3	6, 8, 9
24	3	7, 8, 9
10	4	1, 2, 3, 4
11	4	1, 2, 3, 5
29	4	5, 7, 8, 9
30	4	6, 7, 8, 9
15	5	1, 2, 3, 4, 5
16	5	1, 2, 3, 4, 6
34	5	4, 6, 7, 8, 9
35	5	5, 6, 7, 8, 9

Ninja Notes

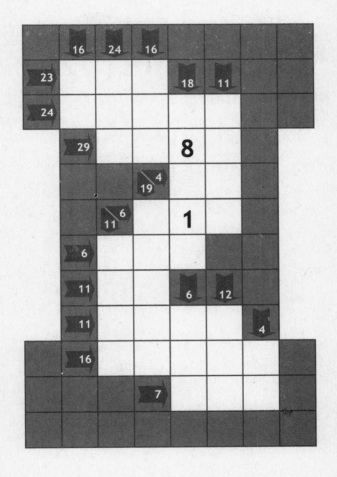

Target	Number of Squares	Combination
3	2	1, 2
4	2	1, 3
16	2	7, 9
17	2	8, 9
6	3	1, 2, 3
7	3	1, 2, 4
23	3	6, 8, 9
24	3	7, 8, 9
10	4	1, 2, 3, 4
11	4	1, 2, 3, 5
29	4	5, 7, 8, 9
30	4	6, 7, 8, 9
15	5	1, 2, 3, 4, 5
16	5	1, 2, 3, 4, 6
34	5	4, 6, 7, 8, 9
35	5	5, 6, 7, 8, 9

Ninja Notes

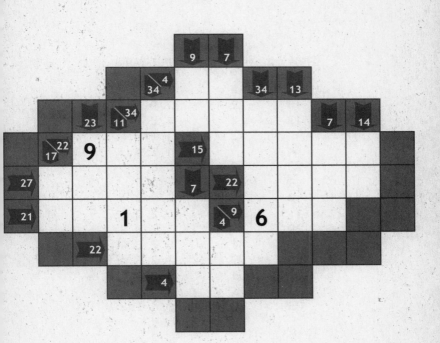

Target	Number of Squares	Combination
3	2	1, 2
4	2	1, 3
16	2	7, 9
17	2	8, 9
6	3	1, 2, 3
7	3	1, 2, 4
23	3	6, 8, 9
24	3	7, 8, 9
10	4	1, 2, 3, 4
11	4	1, 2, 3, 5
29	4	5, 7, 8, 9
30	4	6, 7, 8, 9
15	5	1, 2, 3, 4, 5
16	5	1, 2, 3, 4, 6
34	5	4, 6, 7, 8, 9
35	5	5, 6, 7, 8, 9

Ninja Notes

Target	Number of Squares	Combination
3	2	1, 2
4	2	1, 3
16	2	7, 9
17	2	8, 9
6	3	1, 2, 3
7	3	1, 2, 4
23	3	6, 8, 9
24	3	7, 8, 9
10	4	1, 2, 3, 4
11	4	1, 2, 3, 5
29	4	5, 7, 8, 9
30	4	6, 7, 8, 9
15	5	1, 2, 3, 4, 5
16	5	1, 2, 3, 4, 6
34	5	4, 6, 7, 8, 9
35	5	5, 6, 7, 8, 9

Ninja Notes

Target	Number of Squares	Combination
3	2	1, 2
4	2	1, 3
16	2	7, 9
17	2	8, 9
6	3	1, 2, 3
7	3	1, 2, 4
23	3	6, 8, 9
24	3	7, 8, 9
10	4	1, 2, 3, 4
11	4	1, 2, 3, 5
29	4	5, 7, 8, 9
30	4	6, 7, 8, 9
15	5	1, 2, 3, 4, 5
16	5	1, 2, 3, 4, 6
34	5	4, 6, 7, 8, 9
35	5	5, 6, 7, 8, 9

Ninja Notes

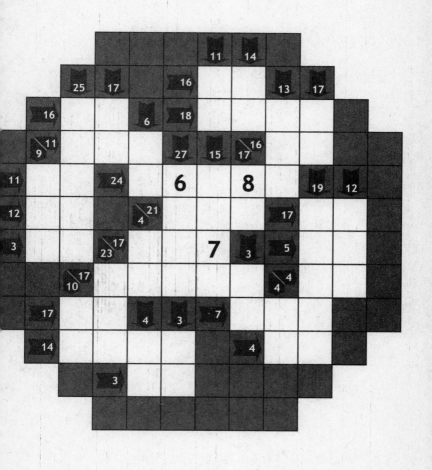

Target	Number of Squares	Combination
3	2	1, 2
4	2	1, 3
16	2	7, 9
17	2	8, 9
6	3	1, 2, 3
7	3	1, 2, 4
23	3	6, 8, 9
24	3	7, 8, 9
10	4	1, 2, 3, 4
11	4	1, 2, 3, 5
29	4	5, 7, 8, 9
30	4	6, 7, 8, 9
15	5	1, 2, 3, 4, 5
16	5	1, 2, 3, 4, 6
34	5	4, 6, 7, 8, 9
35	5	5, 6, 7, 8, 9

Ninja Notes

Target	Number of Squares	Combination
3	2	1, 2
4	2	1, 3
16	2	7, 9
17	2	8, 9
6	3	1, 2, 3
7	3	1, 2, 4
23	3	6, 8, 9
24	3	7, 8, 9
10	4	1, 2, 3, 4
11	4	1, 2, 3, 5
29	4	5, 7, 8, 9
30	4	6, 7, 8, 9
15	5	1, 2, 3, 4, 5
16	5	1, 2, 3, 4, 6
34	5	4, 6, 7, 8, 9
35	5	5, 6, 7, 8, 9

Ninja Notes

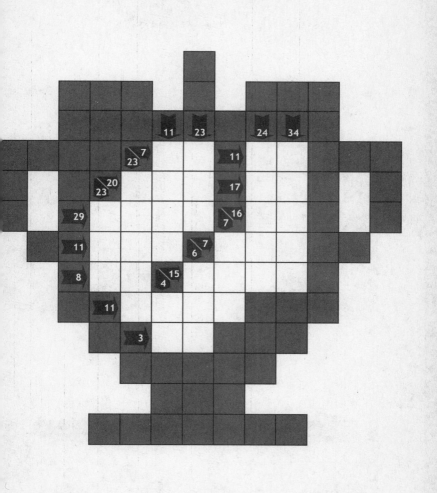

Solutions

1
Starter 1

	2	1			3	1	
	3	6		5	1	2	
		2	1	3			
			5	1	3		
	1	3	2		4	2	
	2	1			1	8	

2
Starter 2

			3	2			
		4	1	5			
	1	2		3	5	2	
	3	1	4		3	1	
			3	1	2		
			2	8			

3
Starter 3

	1	5			4	3	
	3	2	4		1	2	
			5	2	3		
		2	1	6			
	1	3		1	4	3	
	2	5			2	1	

4
Starter 4

			2	1			
			1	3	4		
	2	5	3		3	2	
	3	1		3	2	4	
		2	4	1			
		5	2				

Solutions

5
Slanty Right

6
Slanty Left

7
Button

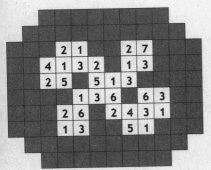

8
"S"

Solutions

9
Rocket

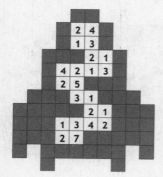

10
White Flag

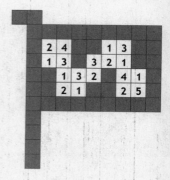

11
Example

12
White Star

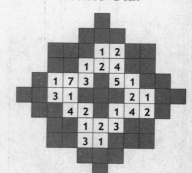

Solutions

13
Zig Zag

14
Car

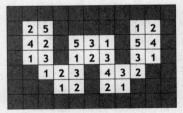

15
Wishbone

16
"W"

17
Column

18
Freestyle

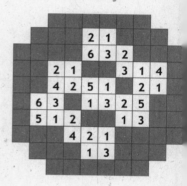

19
Diamond

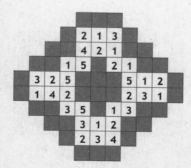

20
Corner

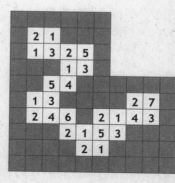

Solutions

21
Rainbow

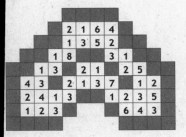

22
Snake

23
Exclamation Mark

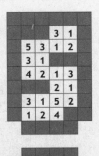

24
Question Mark

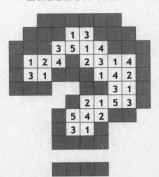

Solutions

25
Yellow Flag

		7	2	4		
	4	2	3	1		
2	1	3		2	4	1
1	3				1	2
4	2	1		4	2	3
		2	1	5	3	
		4	3	2		

26
Box

1	3					2	1
2	1	5	4			4	5
		2	1	5	3		
	2	1		3	1		
	4	3	1	2			
1	3		5		1	4	3
2	1				2	1	

27
Freestyle

		2	6	5			
		4	1	2			
		1	2	3			
	2	3		1	2		
1	3			5	2		
2	1			3	1		
	4	2		3	1		
	1	4	2				
	3	2	1				
	5	1	8				

28
Truck

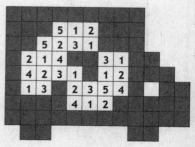

			5	1	2			
		5	2	3	1			
2	1	4			3	1		
4	2	3	1		1	2		
1	3		2	3	5	4		
		4	1	2				

29
Computer

2	6			4	2	1	
1	3		2	1	5	3	
	1	4	3	2			
	1	5	3	2			
5	3	2	1		3	1	
8	1	5			1	2	

30
Mask

	1	2			1	2	4	
4	3	1	2		3	5	2	4
2	1			1	2		1	3
4	5	3	2		4	2	1	3
	2	4	1			1	3	

31
Freestyle

			2	7	4		
			3	1	2		
		3	1		1	3	
2	4	1			2	1	3
3	2					6	1
1	7	3			1	4	2
	1	4	2		1	3	2
			4	1	2		
			1	7	6		

32
Wave

4	5				3	1			
1	3			6	1	2	3	
2	4	1		9	1		4	2	3
	2	4	1	3			1	2
	2	4	1			5	1

Solutions

33
"3"

	2	1	4	
5	3	1	2	
		3	1	
1	2	6	4	
3	1			
2	4	3	1	
		5	2	
3	6	1	4	
1	8	2		

34
Right Arrow

2	4	1	3		1	5	6	
1	2	3	5		3	4	1	2
3	1		2	1	4		3	1
7	5		1	3	2			

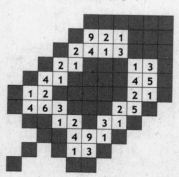

35
Fireworks

36
Teapot

Solutions

37
Cup

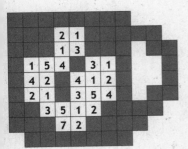

38
"A"

39
"B"

40
"C"

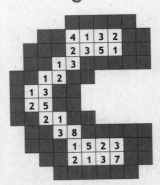

Solutions

41
Moon

2	3	1			
4	5	3	1	2	
			3	1	
		4	2		
3	1	5	4	2	
1	2		1	4	
9	3		3	1	
			1	2	
4	2	1	3		
6	1	3			

42
Rain Cloud

			2	4	1			
		4	1	2	3			
2	4	5	3	1		1	2	
3	1	2		5	2	3	1	
1	2		3	1				

43
Sun

	2	9				
6	3	1	2		3	1
2	1		3	1	5	2
		1	5	2		
5	3	2	1		2	1
2	1		4	2	1	5
		1	3			

44
Dog

					3	1		
				1	2	3		
1	3		3	5		2	7	
2	1	4		4	2	3	1	5
	2	3	4	1		1	4	2
	5	1	3	2				

45
Cat

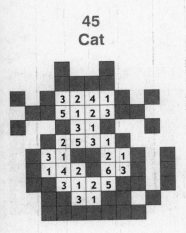

46
Freestyle

47
Freestyle

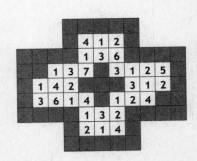

48
Plus

Solutions

49
"N"

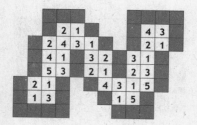

50
Box

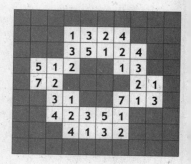

51
Freestyle

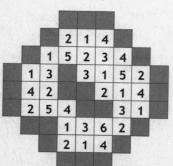

52
T-Shirt

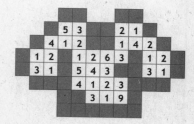

53
Jeans

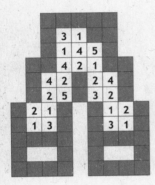

	3	1				
	1	4	5			
	4	2	1			
4	2			2	4	
2	5			3	2	
2	1				1	2
1	3				3	1

54
Slant Right

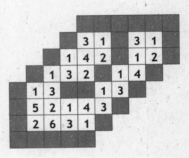

			3	1			3	1
		1	4	2			1	2
		1	3	2		1	4	
	1	3			1	3		
5	2	1	4	3				
2	6	3	1					

55
Green Flag

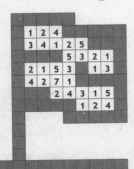

1	2	4			
3	4	1	2	5	
			5	3	2	1
2	1	5	3		1	3
4	2	7	1		
	2	4	3	1	5
		1	2	4	

56
Box

1	3			4	7
2	1	4		8	9
3	5	1	6	2	
4	2		1	3	
		1	3		3	1
		3	2	1	4	5
	1	2		3	1	2
	3	8			9	3

Solutions

57
Boot

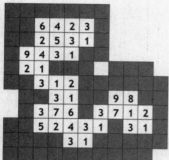

58
Circle

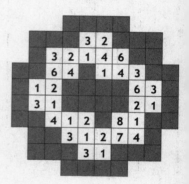

59
Wavy

60
Christmas Tree

61
Snowman

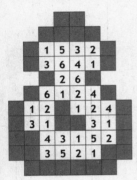

62
Bell

63
Snowflake

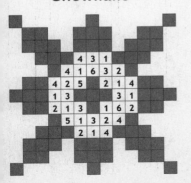

64
Present

Solutions

65
Christmas Stocking

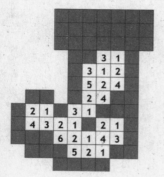

66
Dreidel

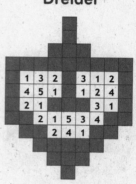

67
Brown Star

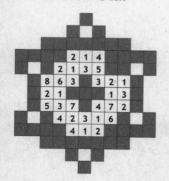

68
Freestyle

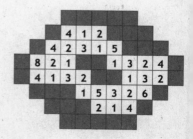

69
Ornament

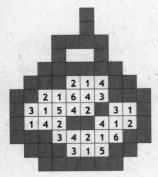

70
Box

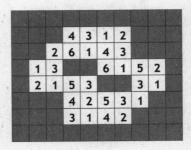

71
Oval

72
Slant Left

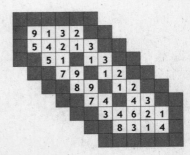

Solutions

73
Light Bulb

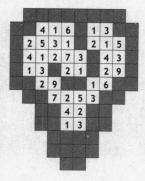

74
Freestyle

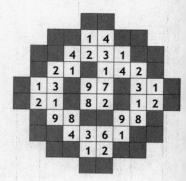

75
Bug

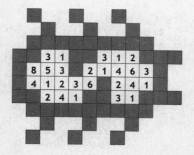

76
"X"

Solutions

77
Staircase

3	1					
1	2					
6	4	2	5			
		3	2	1		
		1	4	2	3	
	3	6	1	5	2	
1	2	4			1	3	5
3	1				4	1	2

78
Box

3	5	2	1			1	2
1	3	4	2			3	1
		1	3	6	5	2	
	1	3	5	4	2		
2	4			2	1	4	5
1	3			1	3	2	7

79
Boat

6	3	1	7			2	1	
2	5	4	3	1		9	2	1	3
3	2	1		5	3	2	1
1	4	2		2	1	4

80
Fish

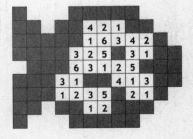

	4	2	1			
	1	6	3	4	2	
3	2	5		3	1	
6	3	1	2	5		
3	1		4	1	3	
1	2	3	5		2	1
	1	2				

81
Jelly Fish

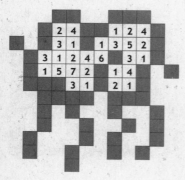

82
One-Ton Weight

83
Pear

84
Freestyle

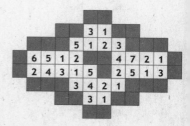

Solutions

85
Spiral

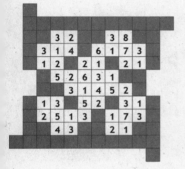

86
Suitcase

87
Balloon

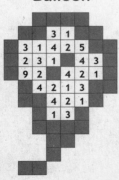

88
"Y"

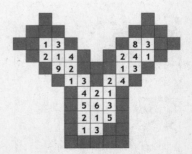

89
"Z"

90
Freestyle

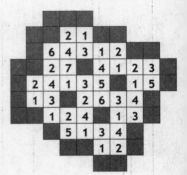

91
Box

92
T.V.